MAYER SMITH

The Forsaken King's Enchanted Bride

Copyright © 2025 by Mayer Smith

All rights reserved. No part of this publication may be reproduced, stored or transmitted in any form or by any means, electronic, mechanical, photocopying, recording, scanning, or otherwise without written permission from the publisher. It is illegal to copy this book, post it to a website, or distribute it by any other means without permission.

This novel is entirely a work of fiction. The names, characters and incidents portrayed in it are the work of the author's imagination. Any resemblance to actual persons, living or dead, events or localities is entirely coincidental.

Mayer Smith asserts the moral right to be identified as the author of this work.

Mayer Smith has no responsibility for the persistence or accuracy of URLs for external or third-party Internet Websites referred to in this publication and does not guarantee that any content on such Websites is, or will remain, accurate or appropriate.

Designations used by companies to distinguish their products are often claimed as trademarks. All brand names and product names used in this book and on its cover are trade names, service marks, trademarks and registered trademarks of their respective owners. The publishers and the book are not associated with any product or vendor mentioned in this book. None of the companies referenced within the book have endorsed the book.

First edition

*This book was professionally typeset on Reedsy.
Find out more at reedsy.com*

Contents

1	The Fateful Encounter	1
2	A Queen's Curse	7
3	Forbidden Power	13
4	The Silent Watcher	20
5	Heart of the Forest	27
6	The Betrayal	34
7	The Blood Moon Rises	41
8	The Shattered King	48
9	The Hidden Sanctuary	54
10	The Veil of Deception	60
11	The Fallen Kingdom	66
12	The Sacrifice	73
13	The Dark Heart	79
14	The Breaking Point	86
15	The Final Choice	92

One

The Fateful Encounter

The wind howled through the ancient trees of the Eldritch Forest, carrying with it a chill that made the hairs on the back of Elara's neck rise. The forest, with its gnarled roots and overgrown thickets, had always felt alive— alive in a way that both frightened and fascinated her. Yet tonight, it was more than that. It pulsed with a strange energy, an unsettling rhythm that spoke of something far darker than the usual mystery the forest offered.

Elara's boots crunched against the fallen leaves as she pushed her way through the underbrush, her breath coming in shallow bursts. The moon was full, casting an eerie light through the dense canopy above, but the shadows it created seemed to deepen rather than lighten the path ahead. She adjusted her cloak, its heavy fabric brushing against her skin, but the cold was seeping through, as if the forest itself were pulling the warmth from her body.

She had come here for a reason, though she could not shake the feeling that this night would not go as planned. The disturbance had been growing for weeks—faint at first, like a whisper in the wind, but now it was undeniable. Something, or someone, was out of place in the heart of the Eldritch Forest. And it was pulling her deeper into its grasp.

"Stay focused," she murmured to herself, her voice barely audible against the wind. Her fingers brushed the hilt of the dagger at her side, the weight of it grounding her in the moment. She had faced danger before. This was no different. Or at least, that was what she told herself.

The path ahead began to narrow, the trees closing in on her. Elara paused, her senses tingling. There was something in the air now, something almost palpable—an oppressive heaviness that made her skin crawl. It wasn't just the usual magic of the forest. This felt… wrong.

A rustle in the distance caught her attention, sharp and sudden. Her breath hitched in her throat as she stilled, every muscle taut. The sound was too deliberate, too purposeful to be the wind. Someone was out there.

She drew her dagger, the steel cold against her palm, and slipped silently between the trees, following the sound. Her footsteps were soundless, her every movement calculated, but the closer she got, the stronger the pull of the dark energy became. It was like a shadow at the edge of her mind, beckoning her forward.

The Fateful Encounter

Then, she saw him.

A figure stood at the edge of a clearing, bathed in the pale light of the moon. He was tall, his back straight, his posture regal even in the solitude of the forest. His cloak billowed around him, dark as the night itself, though it seemed to shimmer with an unnatural sheen. Elara's heart skipped a beat. The figure did not belong to this world—at least, not the one she knew.

She could feel the magic swirling around him, thick and potent, but also... twisted. It was a power unlike anything she had felt before, both alluring and repellent. He was a man out of legend—Kaelen, the Forsaken King.

Her grip tightened around her dagger as she took another step forward, but before she could make her presence known, his head turned, his eyes locking onto hers. The shock of recognition sent a jolt through her body, and for a moment, she froze. His gaze was penetrating, as if he could see into the very core of her being. Those eyes—golden and glowing—held a fire that was both captivating and terrifying.

For a heartbeat, neither of them moved.

Kaelen's lips curled into a knowing smile, and his voice, when it came, was low and smooth, like the sound of silk brushing against skin. "You've been following me for a while now, haven't you?"

Elara's breath caught in her throat. She had been careful, but somehow, this man—this cursed king—had noticed her. How?

The question lingered in her mind, but she could not afford to show weakness. Not now.

"Who are you?" she demanded, her voice steady, though the tremor of fear laced through it. "What do you want?"

Kaelen took a step toward her, the shadows at his feet seeming to stretch and writhe like living things. He was like a shadow himself—both a part of the forest and entirely separate from it. "I could ask you the same thing," he said. "But you already know who I am, don't you, sorceress?"

Elara's pulse quickened, but she refused to back down. She didn't know how he knew, but his knowledge of her was unsettling. "You're nothing but a myth," she spat, trying to hide the uncertainty creeping into her voice. "A king cast out, cursed to walk these woods forever. What could you possibly want with me?"

Kaelen chuckled, a dark, low sound that echoed through the clearing. "A myth, am I?" He took another step, his presence pressing in on her like a physical weight. "I am no myth, sorceress. I am very real. And you... you are exactly what I need."

Elara felt her heart race, her mind spinning with the implications of his words. The weight of his gaze grew heavier, and the magic around them pulsed with a life of its own. She instinctively took a step back, the dagger in her hand raised in defense. "I'm not here to help you."

The Fateful Encounter

He stopped. The air between them thickened, a crackling energy radiating outward, suffocating in its intensity. Kaelen's eyes softened, but there was no kindness in them—only the cold, bitter remnants of a once-proud king brought low by forces beyond his control.

"You don't understand," he said, his voice barely more than a whisper. "The curse I carry is not just mine. It is a part of you, too. Your blood binds you to it."

Elara's stomach dropped, a cold wave of dread crashing over her. Her blood? She had always known there was something about her magic that felt out of place, something darker than what she had been taught. But to hear it from him, to hear it in his voice—it was like a door had been opened to a truth she wasn't ready to face.

Kaelen took another step toward her, his expression unreadable. "You're the one I've been waiting for. The one who can break this curse. The one who can free me."

The words hung in the air between them, heavy with both promise and threat. Elara's mind raced as she processed the implications. He wanted her—no, needed her—to help him break free of the curse. But why her? Why now?

Before she could respond, a low growl broke through the tension. The ground trembled, and Elara spun around, her heart pounding. Shadows seemed to move at the edges of her vision, and from the darkness, shapes began to emerge—creatures she could not identify, but whose hunger was unmistakable.

Kaelen's voice cut through the chaos. "It's not just the curse that hunts me. It's the ones who would see me destroyed."

The creatures closed in around them, and Elara's breath caught in her throat. She had no choice now. She had to fight, had to survive. But even as she prepared for battle, the seed of doubt planted by Kaelen's words took root in her mind. Could he be telling the truth? Could she truly be the key to ending the curse?

As the first creature lunged, Elara struck, her dagger flashing in the moonlight. But even as she fought, she could not shake the feeling that this was just the beginning—and that the true danger, the true test, was yet to come.

Two

A Queen's Curse

The moon hung low in the sky, barely a sliver of pale light amidst the veil of storm clouds. The wind howled through the treetops, carrying with it the distant sound of thunder, like a warning—an omen of things to come. Elara's breath came in shallow gasps as she moved through the winding corridors of Kaelen's hidden refuge, her heart still pounding from the ambush in the forest. The creatures they had fought off had been relentless, but they were gone now, vanquished or scattered by the intense magic that Kaelen had unleashed in defense.

But as the adrenaline slowly faded, Elara couldn't shake the lingering unease that clung to her skin like the damp air. The night had revealed too much, too quickly, and now, in the stillness of the stone chamber, her mind raced with questions—questions Kaelen had refused to answer.

"Do you think they will follow us?" Elara asked, her voice soft but edged with tension as she glanced at Kaelen. He stood by the door, his silhouette framed by the flickering light of a single torch. His face was unreadable, his golden eyes focused on the shadows beyond the threshold. The room was sparse, save for the worn tapestries lining the walls, their colors faded by time and neglect.

Kaelen turned to her, his expression inscrutable. "They will not," he said flatly. "Not tonight."

Elara's brow furrowed. His certainty unsettled her. "You're not worried?"

Kaelen's lips twisted into a faint, sardonic smile. "I've been hunted by worse than shadow creatures for years. A few beasts won't be enough to stop me."

Despite his calm demeanor, Elara could sense something darker lurking beneath the surface. The storm outside was nothing compared to the tempest inside him. She had seen it earlier, when his magic surged out of him in a violent, uncontrollable explosion. It had been a power unlike anything she had ever witnessed, and for a fleeting moment, she had wondered if she had made a grave mistake by aligning herself with him.

"You're not telling me everything," Elara said, the words slipping out before she could stop them. She felt the weight of them as soon as they left her lips. She was walking a fine line—her suspicion growing, but her desire to uncover the truth pushing her forward.

A Queen's Curse

Kaelen's eyes met hers, and for the briefest moment, she saw something vulnerable flicker in them, something that made her breath catch in her throat. Then, it was gone, buried beneath the layers of mystery and pain that surrounded him.

"What would you have me say?" he asked, his voice low and steady, though a slight tremor of uncertainty betrayed him. "That the curse I carry is not only mine, but yours as well? That your blood binds you to the fate of my kingdom? That you are the one who will either break the curse or be consumed by it?"

Elara felt her heart skip a beat. The words hit her like a blow, and she took an instinctive step back, her pulse spiking. "What do you mean, my blood?" She could feel the heat rising in her chest, a mixture of fear and disbelief.

Kaelen's eyes darkened, the golden hue flickering as if the magic within him were reacting to her growing agitation. "You are not just a sorceress, Elara," he said, his voice heavy with the weight of unspoken truths. "Your lineage is bound to the ancient magic that cursed me. To break the curse, to free me… it will require more than your will. It will require something far deeper."

Elara's mind reeled. Her blood? Her heritage had always been a mystery, a tangled web of rumors and half-truths, but this—this was something she had never imagined. She had always known her magic was different, more potent than most. But the idea that her very existence was tied to a curse as ancient and dark as Kaelen's… it was unthinkable.

"What are you saying?" she demanded, her voice shaking. "That

I'm… fated to undo this curse? That I am the key?"

Kaelen's gaze softened, but there was no warmth in it. Only the cold truth of what he had known for so long. "Yes. But not in the way you think. You are not merely a vessel to contain the magic. You are bound to me—through your blood, through the ancient bonds of your ancestors. The curse on my kingdom and my throne was forged long before I was born, and you, Elara, are a part of it. Whether you want to be or not."

Elara took a step back, her mind spinning. This couldn't be true. She couldn't be connected to this man, to this cursed king. She had always fought to stand apart, to be her own person, independent and untethered. But now, it seemed that the very forces that shaped her life were pulling her in a direction she hadn't chosen, one that led her straight into Kaelen's dark world.

"No," she whispered, almost to herself. "This is a mistake. I don't even know you."

Kaelen's expression hardened, the flicker of vulnerability gone. "And yet, here you are," he said quietly, his voice carrying a weight that pressed down on her chest. "You came to me, followed me into this cursed land, and now you are bound to it. To me."

Elara shook her head, trying to clear the fog of confusion and fear. She couldn't—she wouldn't—be part of this twisted fate. She had her own path, her own purpose. She had to find a way out. She had to break free.

A Queen's Curse

Suddenly, the sound of footsteps echoed in the corridor, sharp and hurried. Elara's instincts kicked in, and she reached for the dagger at her side, ready to defend herself. Kaelen's eyes flicked toward the door, his body tensing as he silently gestured for her to be still.

The door swung open with a violent creak, and a figure stepped into the room, cloaked in darkness. Elara's heart skipped, her senses on high alert. The figure was tall, broad-shouldered, and exuded an aura of power that made her pulse race. As the figure stepped into the light, she recognized him immediately.

"Alistair," Kaelen said, his voice low, though there was no warmth in it. "What are you doing here?"

The man—Alistair—smiled, though there was no humor in it. His eyes, dark and piercing, fixed on Elara with a predatory gleam. "I could ask you the same, Kaelen," he said, his tone smooth as velvet, but edged with something darker. "I see you've made a new acquaintance. How... charming."

Elara's grip tightened on her dagger, her pulse quickening as the tension in the room thickened. This man—Alistair—was not here for a friendly chat. He was here with an agenda, and Elara was certain it had nothing to do with breaking curses or ancient bloodlines.

Kaelen's eyes narrowed. "You should not have come, Alistair."

Alistair chuckled, a low, menacing sound. "I think you'll find I'm rather difficult to avoid, my friend."

The room seemed to shrink as the two men locked eyes, their unspoken rivalry crackling in the air. Elara stood frozen between them, caught in the middle of something far more dangerous than she had ever anticipated. She had thought she understood the stakes, but now, with Alistair's arrival, she realized she had only scratched the surface of the deadly game that was unfolding.

She glanced at Kaelen, but his expression was unreadable. She had no idea who this Alistair was, but she could feel the danger radiating from him, the tension in the room thickening with every passing second. Whatever their history, whatever their past, Elara knew one thing for certain: nothing would ever be the same again.

And as the storm outside raged on, she knew that the curse was no longer the only thing she had to fear.

Three

Forbidden Power

The storm raged outside, but inside the dimly lit chamber, a different kind of tension thickened the air. Elara stood by the window, her eyes tracing the jagged lines of lightning that split the sky, the thunder a constant, rumbling threat in the distance. The wind howled through the cracks of the stone walls, but it was the low murmurs of the two men behind her that truly unsettled her.

Kaelen had not spoken since Alistair's arrival, but the tension between them was palpable. Elara could feel it in the way Kaelen's body had stiffened when Alistair entered, in the barely contained hostility that simmered between them. Alistair, for his part, seemed unfazed. He moved about the room with an air of casual superiority, his gaze often flicking toward Elara with a strange, knowing smile that made her skin crawl.

Kaelen was clearly not happy to have him here, but she couldn't help but wonder—why had he come? The question had burned in her mind since Alistair had appeared, but now, with the storm outside and the storm inside the room, it felt as though she might never get the answers she needed.

"Elara," Kaelen's voice cut through the thick silence, and she turned, surprised to hear her name. His golden eyes were watching her with an intensity that made her pulse quicken. "You don't need to stay for this."

Her brow furrowed. "What do you mean?"

Kaelen's gaze flicked toward Alistair, who had just seated himself in a chair by the fire, as if he were completely at ease. His casual arrogance only fueled the unease that was gnawing at her. "You don't need to witness this," Kaelen repeated, his voice lower this time, a warning in his tone. "I'll handle Alistair."

Elara crossed her arms, refusing to be dismissed so easily. "I'm not leaving," she said firmly, meeting Kaelen's gaze. There was no way she would back down now—not after everything that had happened, not after learning what she had about her blood, her connection to this cursed king. No, she wasn't about to let Kaelen—or Alistair—shut her out.

Kaelen's jaw tightened, but before he could respond, Alistair's voice filled the space between them, smooth and unbothered. "Ah, I see. The sorceress has a backbone after all." He chuckled darkly, the sound like a razor's edge. "How quaint."

Elara shot him a glare, but Alistair only grinned wider, as though her disdain amused him. "It's good that you've decided to stay, Elara. It makes things far more… interesting."

Kaelen's expression darkened. "Enough, Alistair."

Alistair raised a hand, as if to calm him, but his smile never faltered. "I'm not the one you need to worry about, Kaelen." His gaze shifted to Elara, and something dangerous flickered in his eyes. "She is."

Elara's blood ran cold. The words hit her like a blow, and her breath caught in her throat. "What do you mean by that?"

Alistair leaned forward, his eyes gleaming with something she couldn't quite place. "You have no idea, do you?" He let out a soft laugh, shaking his head as if she were a child who had yet to learn the harsh realities of the world she had walked into. "You think you're just a pawn in Kaelen's game. But you're not. You are the game."

Elara took a step back, her heart pounding in her chest. "I don't understand," she whispered, more to herself than to him.

Alistair's smile widened. "You will. Soon enough."

Kaelen moved suddenly, his fists clenched at his sides, but it wasn't directed at Alistair. It was as if his own restraint were beginning to crack, the edges of his control fraying with every word Alistair spoke. Elara could feel the tension building in the room, a pressure that threatened to explode at any moment.

She couldn't tell if Kaelen was about to snap at Alistair or if he was on the verge of imploding under the weight of his own emotions.

Kaelen's voice was tight with barely contained fury when he spoke again. "You need to leave, Alistair."

Alistair chuckled, a sound that was equal parts mocking and dark. "Oh, I'm not going anywhere. Not until I'm finished." His gaze slid back to Elara, studying her with a mix of curiosity and amusement. "Kaelen's little secret is that he's not the only one with power. Oh, no. He may have been cursed, but he's not the only one with the means to break it."

Elara's heart skipped a beat. "What are you talking about?"

Alistair's eyes gleamed as he leaned back in his chair. "You see, Kaelen is no ordinary man, no ordinary king. His curse is bound by blood, by ancient magic that runs deeper than even he understands. And the key to that curse? It's not some trinket or artifact, not some hidden relic. It's something far more dangerous." He paused, letting the words hang in the air like poison. "It's power."

Elara took a shaky breath, but she was determined not to let him see her fear. She had faced powerful magic before, but this—this was something entirely different. Something that felt as though it could swallow her whole.

"What are you saying?" she demanded, her voice steady despite the knot of dread in her stomach. "What power?"

Alistair's smile turned cruel. "Kaelen's curse isn't just a simple spell. It's a complex web of magic, designed to bind him to a fate far darker than he could ever imagine. And you, Elara, you're the one who can undo it."

The words hit her like a physical blow. Her breath caught in her throat, and for a moment, she couldn't move. "Me?" she whispered.

Kaelen's eyes flared with anger, his jaw tight as if he were about to lash out. "Don't listen to him," he warned, but Elara's mind was already spinning.

Alistair's smile deepened. "Oh, it's true. The blood that runs through your veins is the only thing capable of undoing the curse. But that's not all. You are connected to the power that created it. The very same power that binds Kaelen to his throne." He leaned forward, his voice dropping to a conspiratorial whisper. "And that power—well, it's not something you can control."

Elara shook her head, her thoughts a whirl of confusion and disbelief. "I don't have power like that."

Alistair's gaze was piercing, his eyes gleaming with cruel satisfaction. "Oh, but you do. You just don't know how to unlock it yet."

The room seemed to close in around her. The storm outside was nothing compared to the storm that was brewing inside. The sense of foreboding, of danger that hung in the air, felt suffocating. Elara's pulse was racing, her thoughts tangled in a web of uncertainty and fear. She had always known there was something different about her, something that set her apart from others, but this… this was far beyond anything she could have imagined.

And then, just as she was about to speak, to demand more answers, Kaelen's voice shattered the tension like a crack of thunder.

"Leave now, Alistair," he commanded, his voice cold, final. "I won't say it again."

Alistair's smile faded, but there was no fear in his eyes. He only stood, his movements slow and deliberate, as if he were savoring the moment. "You'll regret this, Kaelen. You're pushing me too far. Both of you."

With a last, lingering look at Elara, Alistair turned and left the room, the door swinging shut behind him with a heavy thud that echoed in the silence that followed.

Elara stood frozen, the weight of his words settling over her like a heavy cloak. Her mind was a whirl of questions, but none of them seemed to have answers. The room felt smaller now, suffocating in its quiet.

Kaelen remained by the window, his back to her, his fists clenched at his sides. She could feel the tension radiating from him, the tightness in his posture betraying the anger he was barely holding in check. The silence between them stretched,

Forbidden Power

and for a long time, neither spoke.

Finally, Elara broke the stillness. "What did he mean?" Her voice was barely above a whisper, but it cut through the air like a knife. "What power? What blood?"

Kaelen's shoulders sagged, and when he turned to face her, his eyes were filled with a mixture of regret and resignation. "The truth, Elara. The truth you aren't ready to hear."

And with that, the storm outside seemed to roar louder, the skies darkening as if reflecting the growing storm in Elara's heart.

Four

The Silent Watcher

The fire crackled softly in the hearth, its orange glow casting flickering shadows across the stone walls of the chamber. Elara sat in silence, her fingers tracing the rim of the cup before her, the bitter taste of cold tea lingering on her tongue. Her mind, however, was far from the warmth of the fire. Her thoughts were tangled in the web of secrets Kaelen had so carefully woven, and the ominous words Alistair had left hanging in the air.

The power is yours to unlock.

She couldn't shake the feeling that she was standing on the edge of something she couldn't quite see—a precipice where, once she stepped over it, there would be no return. The more she thought about Alistair's cryptic warnings, the more the sense of danger intensified. And yet, even as the storm outside raged, the greatest threat seemed to come not from the world around her, but from within herself.

She pushed her tea aside and stood, pacing the floor. The chamber felt smaller now, the stone walls closing in, heavy with the weight of unanswered questions. Kaelen had barely spoken since Alistair's departure, and when he had, his words were few, curt. The tension between them was thick, palpable. It seemed as though the space between them had become a battleground, one where emotions and suspicions warred silently, and neither was willing to break the silence first.

Her eyes flicked toward him, where he stood at the far end of the room, staring out the window into the darkness. His posture was rigid, and she could feel the barely-contained anger in him, a storm just beneath the surface. The flickering candlelight cast shadows across his face, highlighting the sharp angles of his jaw, the stormy depths of his golden eyes. He was so closed off, so distant, as if he were guarding himself against some unseen force.

Elara took a deep breath and made her way toward him. "Kaelen," she began, her voice soft but firm. "You can't keep shutting me out. I need answers. Alistair's words—they're—"

Kaelen's head snapped toward her, his gaze piercing, the intensity in his eyes like a flame threatening to consume everything in its path. "You need to stay out of this," he growled, his voice low and dangerous. "This is not your fight. You don't know what you're dealing with."

Elara stood her ground, her chest tightening with the weight of his words. "I don't know what I'm dealing with? You brought me into this, Kaelen. I have no choice but to fight. Whether I want to or not."

Kaelen's fists clenched at his sides, and for a brief moment, Elara thought he might lash out. But instead, he turned his back to her, walking toward the far corner of the room, his shoulders stiff with restraint. "I didn't ask you to stay," he muttered, the words barely audible.

A bitter laugh escaped her lips. "No, but you didn't stop me either." She crossed her arms, her frustration mounting. "Tell me what's going on, Kaelen. Why does Alistair want me? What does he mean by all this power?"

There was a long silence, one so thick that Elara thought it might suffocate them both. Finally, Kaelen spoke, his voice quieter now, strained with something she couldn't quite place. "You think you know what's at stake. But you don't. You can't possibly understand the forces at play here."

"And why is that?" Elara's voice was sharp, her patience wearing thin. "Because I'm not cursed? Because I don't have your blood?"

Kaelen's head whipped around, his gaze locking with hers, and there was a flicker of something dark in his eyes. "Don't ever mention my blood again." The words were like a command, and the rawness in his voice struck a chord deep within her.

The Silent Watcher

She flinched but stood her ground. "Then explain it to me. All of it. What is this curse? Why does it have anything to do with me?"

Kaelen's expression faltered for a moment, as though he were on the verge of saying something—something that could change everything. But before he could speak, there was a sharp knock on the door.

Both of them froze.

Elara's heart skipped a beat as the air seemed to thicken, the pulse of magic around them intensifying in a way that sent a chill through her bones. She exchanged a glance with Kaelen, who stood stock-still, his expression unreadable. The knock echoed again, louder this time, insistent.

"Who is it?" Kaelen's voice was a low growl, his eyes narrowed as though he could sense something dangerous on the other side of the door.

"I've come for her," a voice answered, smooth and deadly. "Let her through."

Elara's blood ran cold at the words, her heart hammering in her chest. She didn't recognize the voice, but it was not Kaelen's, and it wasn't Alistair's either. Whoever was outside, they knew her. That much was clear.

Kaelen's eyes flicked toward the door, and his face hardened. "Stay back," he ordered, but his voice betrayed an undercurrent of tension that sent a shiver down Elara's spine.

Before she could respond, Kaelen moved swiftly, crossing the room with a predatory grace that took her by surprise. He reached for the door, and Elara instinctively stepped toward him, but before she could stop herself, the door was pulled open with a violent jerk.

A man stood in the doorway—tall, cloaked in black, his features obscured by a hood, but his eyes... those eyes were like a cold winter's night, empty and endless. There was something about him that made Elara's skin crawl. A predatory gleam in his gaze, a look that spoke of death and darkness, a shadow she could feel pressing against her chest.

"Elara," he said, his voice like velvet, cold and smooth. "I've been watching you."

Kaelen's hand shot out, closing around the man's wrist with a force that made the stranger flinch, but the man didn't seem afraid. In fact, he almost seemed amused.

"You shouldn't be here," Kaelen growled, his voice low and dangerous. "I told you to stay away."

The stranger's lips curled into a grin, though it didn't reach his eyes. "You cannot control me, Kaelen," he said softly. "Not anymore. The time is coming."

Kaelen's grip tightened, and for a brief moment, the air between them crackled with magic. But the man did not flinch. Instead,

The Silent Watcher

he tilted his head to one side, watching them both with the detached curiosity of someone who had seen this play out a thousand times before.

"Elara," he said again, his gaze flicking to her, and this time, there was no mistaking the hunger in his eyes. "I've come to take you with me."

The words hung in the air, a threat, a promise, and Elara's heart pounded in her chest as she instinctively reached for her dagger. But the stranger's smile only widened, and before she could react, the room seemed to grow colder, the shadows pressing in closer.

Kaelen moved before she could do anything, his hand lifting the man by the throat, his magic flaring with a surge of raw power that sent a tremor through the room. "You're not taking her," he snarled.

The stranger's laugh was dark and low, filled with a kind of cruel amusement. "You can't protect her forever, Kaelen. The curse is already in motion. She will come to us. You can't stop it."

Kaelen's eyes flashed with fury, but Elara felt a strange pull in her chest—a cold weight, a force that was no longer just around them, but in them. It was like the room itself was alive, a pressure closing in from all sides.

"Who are you?" Elara's voice trembled as she stepped forward, her hand shaking on the dagger at her side.

The stranger's smile never faltered. "A watcher. Someone who has been waiting for you."

And with those words, the world around them seemed to shift, as though the very air had thickened, charged with magic. The man released a breathless chuckle, and before either Kaelen or Elara could react, he stepped backward, disappearing into the shadows with a swiftness that left her heart racing and her thoughts reeling.

The door slammed shut with a finality that echoed through the room.

Kaelen's grip on the air around them remained tight, his golden eyes flashing with fury, but beneath it, there was something else—something deeper. Something that spoke of a past he hadn't yet revealed.

Elara could only stand there, her breath shallow, her pulse racing. The shadows were still there, lingering, as if the watcher had left a part of himself behind.

But one thing was clear: whoever they were, they were coming for her.

Five

Heart of the Forest

The moonlight filtered through the dense canopy of trees above, casting an eerie glow over the path that wound through the heart of the Eldritch Forest. The air was thick with the scent of damp earth and moss, a fragrance both familiar and unsettling. Elara's breath came in sharp, shallow bursts, her feet moving swiftly over the uneven ground, guided only by the faint glow of her lantern and the steady pulse of magic thrumming in her veins.

Kaelen walked beside her, his presence like a shadow, silent and brooding. She could feel the tension radiating from him, the barely contained storm beneath his calm exterior. Every step he took seemed deliberate, as though he was prepared for something—something he hadn't shared with her yet. She wanted to ask, wanted to demand the truth, but something held her back. She couldn't shake the feeling that the deeper they went into the forest, the closer they came to uncovering something that neither of them was ready to face.

"Are we close?" Elara asked, her voice low, her words swallowed by the dense foliage around them.

Kaelen didn't answer immediately. Instead, he stopped, his head tilting slightly as he listened to the sounds of the forest. The wind rustled the leaves above, and the distant call of a nightbird echoed through the trees, but beneath it all, there was something else—a whispering, a faint murmur of voices that Elara couldn't quite catch. She frowned, her hand instinctively reaching for the dagger at her waist, her senses heightened.

"Not far," Kaelen said finally, his voice a murmur in the stillness of the night. "But we must be careful. The heart of this forest holds more than just ancient magic."

Elara glanced at him, her brow furrowing. "What do you mean?"

Kaelen's golden eyes flicked to hers, his gaze sharp, but there was something else in it—a warning. "There are forces here older than you can imagine. And they don't take kindly to trespassers."

The unease in his voice only deepened her sense of foreboding. What had they come here to find? What was waiting for them in the heart of this cursed place?

They continued walking in silence, the thick trees closing in around them, the shadows growing longer, darker. The further they ventured, the more oppressive the air became, as though the forest itself was pressing in on them, alive with a dark, ancient power. The pulse of magic was stronger now, almost overwhelming, but it was mixed with something else—something more dangerous. Elara's heart raced as she felt the weight of it, the pull of something hidden in the depths of the forest.

Suddenly, a flicker of movement caught her eye. She turned sharply, her lantern swinging as she searched the shadows. But there was nothing—nothing but the whispering wind and the rustling leaves.

Kaelen stopped beside her, his body tensing, his eyes narrowing as he scanned the surrounding darkness. "We're not alone," he murmured, his voice low and dangerous.

Elara's pulse quickened. "Who's out there?" she demanded, her hand gripping the hilt of her dagger tightly.

Kaelen raised a hand, signaling for her to remain still. "No one who should be here."

The air around them seemed to hum with energy, the magic in the forest intensifying, until Elara felt as though the very earth beneath her feet was vibrating. She could hear the faintest of whispers now, like a chorus of voices, chanting in a language she couldn't understand. The words were foreign, yet they tugged at something deep within her, a forgotten part of herself that stirred uneasily.

Without warning, Kaelen stepped forward, his movements swift and purposeful. "This way," he commanded, his voice carrying an authority that left no room for argument. Elara hesitated for only a moment before following him, her steps faltering as the forest seemed to shift around them. The trees grew closer, their twisted branches reaching out like skeletal hands, and the path ahead narrowed, disappearing into the darkness.

The whispers grew louder, more insistent, swirling around her like a thousand voices pressing in from all directions. Her breath caught in her throat as she struggled to make sense of the sound. It wasn't just magic—it was something older, something far more primal.

"Kaelen..." Elara whispered, her voice trembling. "What's happening?"

Kaelen didn't answer. Instead, he moved with purpose, his focus unwavering as he pressed forward. They reached a clearing, and for a moment, Elara thought they had reached the heart of the forest. The air was thick with an unnatural stillness, the trees surrounding them like silent sentinels. In the center of the clearing stood an altar—a stone structure, ancient and worn, its surface etched with symbols that seemed to shift in the dim light.

Elara's heart skipped a beat as she approached the altar, her eyes tracing the carvings on the stone. They were familiar, somehow, though she couldn't place where she had seen them before. The symbols seemed to pulse with the same dark magic that had followed them into the forest, the same power that now wrapped around her like a suffocating cloak.

"This is it," Kaelen said, his voice a whisper, but his words held a finality that made Elara's stomach tighten with dread. "This is where the curse began."

Elara's gaze shot to him, her eyes wide with shock. "The curse?"

Kaelen nodded, his face grim. "It's here, Elara. This altar holds the key to everything—the key to my kingdom's downfall, to the power that binds us both." He stepped forward, his hand brushing over the cold stone, and the air around them seemed to crackle with magic. The whispers were louder now, more frantic, as though the very forest was alive with anticipation.

Elara's chest tightened as she stepped closer to him, her heart pounding in her ears. She could feel the weight of the magic pressing in on them, a force so strong it was almost suffocating. She could barely breathe, barely think. The symbols on the altar began to glow faintly, and for a moment, Elara thought she saw them shift, rearranging themselves before her eyes.

Suddenly, a sharp sound broke the stillness—a snap of branches, a rustle of movement in the shadows. Elara spun around, her heart leaping in her chest as she drew her dagger, her body tensing in preparation for an attack. But there was nothing there—nothing but the empty darkness of the forest.

"Who's there?" she called, her voice steady despite the fear coiling in her stomach.

Kaelen stepped closer to her, his body tense, his eyes scanning the surroundings. "They've found us."

Elara's breath caught in her throat as figures emerged from the shadows, their movements swift and silent. Dark cloaks billowed around them, their faces obscured by hoods, but Elara could feel their eyes on her, cold and calculating. There were five of them—silent, dangerous, and far too close.

Kaelen's body went rigid beside her, and she could feel the surge of magic rising within him, an almost tangible force that crackled in the air. "You shouldn't be here," he growled, his voice laced with fury.

One of the figures stepped forward, and Elara's breath caught as he threw back his hood. His eyes were dark, void of any warmth, and his smile was twisted with malice. "Oh, but we are, Kaelen. We've been waiting for this moment."

Elara's stomach turned. She knew this man. She had seen him before—his face, his eyes. He was the one who had been watching her. The one who had spoken of her power.

"You," she whispered, her voice barely audible.

The man's smile deepened, his gaze sliding to her with a hungry gleam. "Yes, Elara. It's you we've been waiting for."

A cold wave of fear washed over her as the darkness around them seemed to press in tighter. The forest had become a prison, the air thick with magic and danger. And as the man's words sank in, Elara realized with a sickening certainty that there was no way out. The heart of the forest had found them—and they were no longer safe.

Six

The Betrayal

The winds howled through the cracks in the stone walls, rattling the windows of the ancient tower where Elara and Kaelen had taken refuge. The storm outside raged, but within the confines of the fortress, the air was thick with something far more dangerous than the tempest above. Tension hung in the air like a suffocating blanket, and Elara could feel it pressing down on her chest, suffocating her thoughts.

She had never felt so exposed. So... vulnerable. The words of the shadowy figure in the forest still echoed in her mind, their meaning gnawing at the edges of her consciousness. *It's you we've been waiting for.*

They had made it back to the tower in one piece, but that did nothing to ease the gnawing unease that had settled in her bones. The altar in the heart of the forest had left them with

The Betrayal

more questions than answers. Who were those cloaked figures? What did they want with her? And most of all—why had Kaelen been so eager to get her out of the clearing before they could learn the truth?

She glanced over at him now, standing by the window, his back to her, staring out into the storm. The storm outside mirrored the turmoil inside him, she could feel it. The same darkness that had followed them into the forest seemed to be drawing nearer. She had tried to push him for answers since they'd returned, but every time, he had deflected her questions, his answers cryptic and guarded. It was as though he wanted to shield her from something—a part of the truth he wasn't ready to share.

But she couldn't wait any longer. She needed to know.

"Elara," Kaelen's voice broke through her thoughts, low and strained. He didn't turn to face her, but his tone was enough to send a shiver down her spine. "We can't keep doing this."

She took a step forward, her heart pounding as she approached him. "What do you mean?"

His shoulders stiffened, and she could almost feel the weight of the world resting on them. He finally turned, his golden eyes dark, filled with something she couldn't quite place—guilt, perhaps. Or something deeper, something more dangerous.

"We're playing a game we can't win, Elara," he said, his voice quiet, almost a whisper. "There's no way out of this."

The words hit her like a blow. No way out. The weight of them pressed against her chest, choking her. For a moment, she couldn't breathe.

"What are you saying?" Her voice trembled, but she fought to keep the panic from creeping in. "Kaelen, you have to tell me the truth. You've been keeping something from me—something I don't understand. I can't keep walking in the dark."

He closed his eyes for a moment, his expression strained. "You wouldn't believe me if I told you," he murmured, his voice barely audible.

Elara's breath hitched. "Try me."

Kaelen's eyes snapped open, and there was a flash of something dark in them. Something raw and primal. He stepped closer to her, and for the briefest moment, Elara was certain he was about to break. But then, just as quickly, he withdrew, turning away again.

"I don't want you involved in this," he said, his voice hardening. "You're better off leaving now, Elara. While you still can."

The words stung. "You don't get to decide that," she spat, her fists clenched at her sides. "I'm already involved, Kaelen. Whether you like it or not."

His gaze met hers, and there was a flicker of pain in his eyes. "You don't know what you're asking for. This curse—this magic—it's more than just a spell. It's a force, one that has

The Betrayal

destroyed everything it touched. If you stay with me, you'll be dragged into it. I won't let that happen."

Elara's heart twisted in her chest. "I'm not afraid of you, Kaelen," she said, her voice barely a whisper. "I'm not afraid of the curse. But I can't live like this. Not knowing. Not when there's a part of me that's already tied to all of this."

She expected him to argue. To tell her to leave again. But instead, he stood there, his expression unreadable, as if he had already given up.

Then, as if to confirm her worst fear, there was a sharp knock at the door.

The sound was sudden, jarring in the heavy silence that had settled between them. Elara's heart skipped a beat, and she turned toward the door, her breath catching in her throat. Who could it be at this hour, in the middle of the storm?

Kaelen's eyes flashed with something dark. "Stay back," he warned, his voice hard as steel.

But Elara was already moving, her instincts kicking in. Whoever was outside, she had no intention of hiding. She needed to know. She needed answers.

The door swung open before Kaelen could stop her.

Standing in the doorway was a figure she didn't recognize—tall, cloaked, and with a presence that seemed to fill the entire room.

His features were hidden beneath a hood, but Elara could feel his gaze on her, cold and calculating.

"I see you've made yourself comfortable," the figure said, his voice low, smooth. But there was something chilling in it, something that sent a ripple of unease through her.

Kaelen's stance shifted. "What do you want?"

The stranger's lips twisted into a smile, but it didn't reach his eyes. "Oh, it's not what I want, Kaelen. It's what you owe."

At that, the figure stepped forward, crossing the threshold into the room without invitation. Elara instinctively moved closer to Kaelen, her eyes narrowing as she watched the stranger carefully. There was a tension in the air now, thick and suffocating, and she could feel the weight of impending danger pressing down on them both.

"What do you owe?" Kaelen repeated, his voice edged with warning.

The figure's gaze flicked to Elara, and for a moment, Elara thought she saw recognition in his eyes. But then it was gone, replaced by something colder.

"A debt," the stranger said, "long overdue."

Before Elara could react, Kaelen moved. His hand shot out, grabbing the figure by the wrist, his grip tight enough to bruise. "You should have stayed away," Kaelen growled, his voice laced

The Betrayal

with barely contained fury.

The stranger didn't flinch. Instead, his lips curled into an almost pitying smile. "You think you control this, Kaelen? You think you control me?" He chuckled darkly, the sound echoing in the stone room. "You're mistaken."

Kaelen's jaw clenched, and for a moment, Elara saw something flicker in his eyes—a darkness she had never seen before. It wasn't just anger. It was something deeper. Something far more dangerous.

"What do you want from me?" Kaelen demanded again, his voice dangerously quiet.

The stranger shrugged, as though the answer was obvious. "What I've always wanted," he said. "What's mine."

Elara took a step forward, her heart racing. "Who are you?"

The figure finally removed his hood, revealing a face that was both unfamiliar and yet hauntingly familiar. His features were sharp, his expression cold, and his eyes—those dark, soulless eyes—locked onto hers.

"You don't recognize me?" he asked, his voice almost amused. "How disappointing."

It took a moment for her to place him, but when she did, the shock hit her like a wave.

It was a name she hadn't heard in years—a name that had been buried in her past, hidden away for her protection. A name that now threatened to unravel everything.

"Dorian," she whispered, the realization sinking in. The betrayal ran deeper than she could have ever imagined.

Seven

The Blood Moon Rises

The moon hung heavy in the sky, its eerie crimson hue casting an unsettling glow over the land. The storm that had raged for days had finally subsided, but in its wake, an oppressive silence had settled over the world—a silence that seemed to hum with an unnatural tension. The forest, still wet with the remnants of the storm, seemed to pulse with energy, its shadows deeper, more foreboding than ever before.

Elara stood at the edge of the clearing, her heart pounding in her chest, her breath coming in sharp, uneven bursts. The air felt thick, suffocating, as though the very earth was holding its breath, waiting for something. She could feel the pull of the magic, the raw power that had begun to stir deep within her, a power she didn't fully understand. It was like a fire in her veins, warm and terrifying, begging to be unleashed.

Beside her, Kaelen stood motionless, his eyes fixed on the sky. His expression was unreadable, but the tension in his body was unmistakable. He, too, felt it—the energy in the air, the weight of the moment. The Blood Moon was upon them, and with it, the curse that had bound him for so long was rising once again.

"Elara," Kaelen's voice was low, almost strained, as he spoke, though he didn't take his eyes off the moon. "When it rises, there's no turning back."

The words hit her like a physical blow. She had known the Blood Moon was coming, but hearing him say it out loud made the reality of it feel inescapable. The curse, the magic, the danger—it was all converging now, and she could feel the walls closing in around her. Every instinct screamed at her to run, to escape before it was too late. But something in her refused to move, refused to back away from the truth.

"What do you mean?" she asked, her voice barely a whisper. "What happens when it rises?"

Kaelen turned to face her then, his golden eyes flickering with an intensity that sent a chill down her spine. "The curse will grow stronger," he said. "And so will the power within you."

Elara's stomach twisted at his words, but she didn't look away. "What power?" she demanded, her voice sharper than she intended. "You keep saying I have power, that it's tied to this curse, but you've never told me what it means. What am I supposed to do?"

The Blood Moon Rises

Kaelen's gaze softened for a moment, but only for a brief moment. His expression was torn—caught between a desire to protect her and the crushing weight of everything he had carried for so long. "I can't tell you everything," he said, his voice thick with regret. "Not yet."

The air around them seemed to crackle with energy, the pulse of magic growing stronger, more insistent. The Blood Moon was rising higher, casting its blood-red light across the land, painting everything in its unnatural glow. Elara could feel it now—the magic within her, swirling, thrumming with power. It was a part of her, yet it felt alien, dangerous, like a fire she couldn't control.

"Kaelen," she said, her voice trembling, though she tried to keep it steady. "What happens to me? To us? When it's too late?"

His eyes met hers, and for a moment, the vulnerability in his gaze broke through the walls he had so carefully built around himself. "I don't know," he admitted, his voice a hushed whisper. "But I know it will change everything. The curse is tied to you now, and the longer you're here, the more you become part of it."

A sudden gust of wind swept through the clearing, snapping Elara back to the present. The shadows around them seemed to shift, moving in unnatural ways, and the ground beneath her feet trembled ever so slightly. The magic in the air was growing heavier, pressing down on them with increasing force, and Elara's pulse quickened as she realized that the moment they had both feared was upon them.

Without warning, a figure emerged from the trees at the edge of the clearing. Tall, cloaked in shadows, his presence a dark stain against the blood-red backdrop of the moon. Elara's heart skipped a beat, and she instinctively took a step back, her hand going to the dagger at her side. She had felt his presence before, the cold, predatory energy that seemed to cling to him like a shroud.

The figure stepped forward, and Elara's breath caught in her throat as he lowered his hood, revealing a face she had only seen in her nightmares. Dorian. The man who had once been her ally. The man who had betrayed her.

"Elara," he said, his voice smooth, like honey, but there was an edge to it now, something darker. "It's time."

Kaelen's body stiffened beside her, and his hand moved to his own weapon. "What do you want, Dorian?" he growled, his voice low and dangerous.

Dorian's smile was cruel, but there was no humor in it. "What I've always wanted," he said. "What's mine."

Elara felt a cold shiver run down her spine. "What do you mean, what's yours?" she demanded, her voice tight with fear and confusion.

Dorian's gaze flicked to her, and for a moment, something almost human seemed to flicker in his eyes—a shadow of regret, perhaps, or a glimmer of something more dangerous. But it was gone in an instant, replaced by a cold, calculating look. "You are a part of something far greater than you realize, Elara," he said, his tone low and dangerous. "And now, it's time for you to claim your place."

Before she could react, Dorian raised his hand, and the air around them seemed to shimmer, a ripple of dark magic that sent a wave of dizziness through Elara. The ground trembled again, more violently this time, and she staggered, clutching at Kaelen's arm for support. She could feel the power in the air, surging, crackling with raw energy, and it was all focused on her.

"What are you doing?" she demanded, her voice rising in panic.

Dorian didn't answer at first. Instead, he stepped closer, his gaze fixed on her, and for the first time, she saw the full weight of the darkness in his eyes. "The power that binds you to this curse," he said, his voice like a hiss, "is the same power that binds me. We are connected, Elara. And tonight, under the Blood Moon, you will either accept your fate… or you will perish."

Elara's heart raced, her pulse pounding in her ears as the magic in the air seemed to close in around her, suffocating her. She could feel it now, deep within her, the power that had been growing inside her for so long. It was a storm, a wild, uncontrollable force, and it was tearing at the fabric of her being.

"Kaelen," she gasped, her voice barely a whisper. "I can't control it."

Kaelen's grip tightened around her arm, his eyes locked on Dorian with a burning intensity. "You don't have to," he said, his voice fierce. "We'll stop him. We'll stop all of this."

But Dorian's laugh rang out, cold and mocking. "You can't stop it, Kaelen," he said, his voice dripping with malice. "It's already too late. The curse has already begun its work. And now, Elara must choose."

The shadows around them seemed to grow darker, the magic swelling with a power that was almost unbearable. Elara's mind raced, her thoughts a blur of fear and confusion. What was she supposed to do? How could she choose when she didn't even understand what was happening to her?

The Blood Moon rose higher, its crimson light bathing the clearing in an unnatural glow. The magic in the air reached a fever pitch, and for a moment, Elara thought she might drown in it.

And then, without warning, everything stopped.

The air went still, the tension in the clearing hanging in the balance. Elara's heart hammered in her chest, her breath coming in shallow gasps as she struggled to make sense of what had just happened.

Kaelen's grip on her arm loosened, and he stepped forward, his eyes never leaving Dorian. "This ends now."

Dorian's lips curled into a smile, but there was no triumph in it.

The Blood Moon Rises

"No," he said softly. "This is only the beginning."

And with those words, the world seemed to tilt on its axis, and Elara realized with a sickening clarity that whatever choice lay before her, there was no escaping the darkness that had already begun to rise.

Eight

The Shattered King

The moon had reached its zenith, casting its blood-red glow across the barren landscape, as though the heavens themselves were marking the moment. Elara stood on the edge of the cliff, the wind biting against her skin, her hair whipping around her face. Below her, the dark expanse of the forest stretched out like a sea of shadows, the trees twisting and shifting in the unnatural light of the Blood Moon.

Her heart raced in her chest, the weight of everything crashing down on her. The power that had been growing inside her—the power she had been trying to understand—was no longer just a whisper. It was a roar, a wildfire that surged through her veins, threatening to consume her from within. And all the while, Kaelen's face lingered in her mind, his eyes filled with unspoken words, his body tense with a barely controlled fury.

The Shattered King

"Do you feel it?" The voice cut through the darkness, sharp and hollow, like a distant echo. Elara turned quickly, her hand instinctively reaching for the dagger at her side, but there was no one there. Only the trees, their branches reaching out like skeletal hands.

But the voice had come from behind her.

She whirled around to find Kaelen standing a few paces away, his figure framed against the blood-red sky. His gaze was locked on her, his expression unreadable, but there was something in the way he stood—something that made her pulse quicken, her body tense with anticipation. He had been distant, colder than she had ever seen him, ever since Dorian's revelation about their shared connection to the curse.

"Kaelen," Elara called out, her voice strained as she stepped toward him. "Kaelen, please. You have to explain—what's happening? What are we supposed to do?"

His eyes flickered to her for a brief moment, and then back to the horizon. The storm in his eyes was palpable, the fury that had been building for so long threatening to break free. For a moment, Elara thought he might speak, might give her the answers she so desperately needed. But instead, he took a deep breath and said nothing.

"Why won't you tell me?" she asked, her voice rising in frustration. "Why won't you trust me?"

Kaelen's jaw tightened, and he turned toward her, his eyes dark and filled with an intensity that almost knocked the breath out of her. He took a step forward, closing the distance between them, but he didn't touch her. Instead, he locked his gaze with hers, as though trying to convey something, something he could never say with words.

"Do you know what it's like to lose everything?" he asked, his voice barely a whisper. "To feel as though your very soul has been torn apart, piece by piece, and there's no way to fix it? Do you have any idea what that's like?"

Elara's heart clenched at the rawness in his voice. She wanted to reach out to him, to offer him the comfort he so clearly needed, but something stopped her. The weight of his words hung in the air between them, a wall she wasn't sure she could breach.

"I..." she began, but the words caught in her throat. What could she say? How could she help him when she was just as lost, just as caught in the web of the curse that had already ensnared them both?

Kaelen turned away from her, his fist clenched at his side. "You don't understand," he muttered, more to himself than to her. "You can't."

But Elara wasn't willing to let him shut her out, not again. Not when they were so close to the truth, to the answers she so desperately needed. She took a step forward, her hand reaching out to him, but the moment her fingers brushed his arm, he flinched, pulling away from her touch as though it burned.

"Don't," he said sharply, his voice cracking. "You can't help me. You don't know what this curse has done to me, to everything I once was."

His words were like ice in her veins, freezing her in place. She knew he was hiding something—something deep and dark, something that had been buried for years. But what was it? What had the curse taken from him?

"I want to understand," she said softly, her voice barely a whisper. "I want to help you, Kaelen."

He didn't look at her, but his body was tense, his back rigid with the weight of some invisible burden. The air around them seemed to crackle with tension, the blood-red glow of the moon casting long shadows across the land. The world felt different now, as though the very ground beneath their feet was shifting, tilting toward something inevitable.

A low growl of thunder echoed in the distance, and Elara turned toward the sound, her heart skipping a beat. The storm was returning, but this time, it was different. The air felt thick, charged with a raw, uncontrollable power.

She glanced back at Kaelen, her pulse racing. Something was wrong. The air was electric with magic, the same magic she had felt growing inside her, the same power that had been calling to her, urging her to embrace it. But Kaelen... He wasn't himself. The man standing before her wasn't the same man who had once been a king. His features were drawn, his expression hollow, and his eyes... His eyes were filled with a despair that cut through her like a blade.

"Kaelen," she whispered, stepping closer. "What happened to you?"

His eyes flicked to hers, a flash of something dark and painful crossing his face before he quickly turned away, his body rigid with tension. The blood-red light of the moon reflected off the edges of his sharp features, casting them in an otherworldly glow. The air was thick, and Elara could feel the power building, the curse rippling through the very ground beneath them.

"Do you see it now?" Kaelen's voice was strained, like it came from a deep, hidden place. "Do you see the price of this magic?"

Elara's stomach dropped. "What price?" she asked, but her voice trembled.

"The price of the throne," Kaelen replied bitterly. "The price of the curse. The price of losing everything."

Before Elara could respond, the air seemed to shudder, and the ground beneath them trembled with an unnatural force. She gasped, instinctively reaching out to Kaelen, but before she could touch him, the world exploded in a wave of searing, blinding light.

The ground buckled beneath them, the world tilting sideways as if the very earth was coming apart at the seams. Elara screamed, her vision clouding as the magic surged around them, a wild storm of power that tore through her, threatening to rip her apart.

Kaelen's voice echoed in her mind, distant and fading. "I never wanted this… Never wanted to be the monster."

Then, as quickly as it had begun, the magic ceased. The world settled into an eerie stillness, the air heavy and thick with the scent of burning wood and earth. Elara's knees buckled, and she collapsed to the ground, gasping for breath as the magic faded, leaving her disoriented and weak.

She looked up, but Kaelen was gone.

Panic surged through her as she scrambled to her feet, her eyes searching the clearing, but there was no sign of him. The Blood Moon hung high in the sky, its red light bathing the land in an unnatural glow, but Kaelen… Kaelen had vanished.

"Elara," a voice called out, faint but clear.

She spun toward the sound, but there was no one there—only the empty expanse of the cliff and the shifting shadows in the distance.

A cold chill ran through her as she realized the truth: The curse had already claimed him. And now, she was truly alone.

Nine

The Hidden Sanctuary

The air was thick with the scent of damp earth and decay. A low fog clung to the forest floor, twisting around the gnarled roots of ancient trees that stretched into the heavens like skeletal fingers. Elara's breath came in sharp, shallow gasps, her heart hammering in her chest as she moved cautiously through the undergrowth. Every step felt like a betrayal of the silence that surrounded her, each footfall too loud, too revealing. The path ahead was barely visible, swallowed by the darkness of the woods, yet Elara felt an undeniable pull to continue forward.

She didn't know how long she had been walking. Hours, maybe days, had passed since the Blood Moon had risen and Kaelen had disappeared, swallowed by the very curse that had haunted him for so long. The world felt as though it was crumbling around her, and with each passing moment, the weight of that uncertainty became unbearable. The power that had been stirring inside her, the magic that she had once thought she could control, now felt like a raging storm, threatening to consume everything in its path.

She couldn't shake the feeling that the very forest was watching her, waiting for her to make a choice. The trees seemed to lean closer, their twisted branches reaching out like hands, their shadows more oppressive with each passing step.

"Elara," a voice called, sharp and familiar.

Her pulse quickened. She froze, her breath catching in her throat. She had been alone—she was certain of it. But there, just beyond her vision, a figure moved through the mist, stepping into the clearing.

"Elara."

The voice was Kaelen's, yet it was distorted, broken, as though it came from some distant place. The figure before her was not Kaelen, but it was unmistakably him—his presence lingered in the air like a heavy weight. She blinked rapidly, willing the vision to clear, but the figure remained, a dark silhouette framed by the ethereal glow of the fog.

"Elara, you have to come to me."

The voice was softer now, pleading, yet there was an edge to it—something darker beneath the surface. The figure's outline began to shift, rippling in the moonlight as if it were made of smoke.

"Elara…" It whispered her name again, this time with a sense of urgency. "Please, you don't understand. The curse, it's too strong. You have to find it before it consumes you."

A chill ran down her spine. The voice was unmistakable now—it was Kaelen. But his words… They made no sense. What was he trying to tell her? And where had he gone? Why had he left her here, alone, in the heart of the forest?

She stumbled back, her pulse racing, her chest tight with fear. "Kaelen?" Her voice trembled, but she wasn't sure if she was speaking to the figure before her or to the ghost of him that lingered in the air. "Where are you?"

The figure before her flickered and shimmered, its edges warping like a mirage. It was as if it was being pulled away from her by some unseen force, and then, as quickly as it had appeared, it was gone, vanished into the fog. The forest around her felt still, impossibly still, as if it, too, was holding its breath.

"Elara…" Kaelen's voice whispered again, fainter this time. "You must find it. The sanctuary… the heart of the curse."

The fog thickened around her, swallowing the clearing, and Elara's heart pounded in her chest. Find it? She had no idea what he was talking about, what this sanctuary was, or how it related to the curse. But something deep inside her—the same force that had pulled her forward all this time—urged her onward.

The Hidden Sanctuary

She had no choice.

Taking a deep breath, she stepped forward into the thickening fog, her senses heightened, her body tense. The air around her felt heavy, thick with the weight of ancient magic. She moved quickly, her feet sinking into the soft earth as she wove through the trees. The whispering in the forest grew louder, the voices of the past and future mingling in the winds, their words lost in the rustling leaves. The magic in the air was palpable, pressing against her skin, pulling her deeper into the forest, deeper into the unknown.

The path ahead became narrower, more treacherous. The trees grew thicker, their branches clawing at her, the roots rising from the ground like serpents waiting to strike. She stumbled, catching herself against a nearby tree, her breath coming in ragged gasps. The darkness seemed to grow heavier with each step, and the air tasted of ash and salt.

And then, as she rounded a bend in the path, she saw it.

A structure loomed before her, half-hidden in the shadows of the trees. It was ancient, its stone walls covered in moss and creeping ivy, its edges worn by time. It was as though the very earth had swallowed it whole, burying it beneath layers of history. A sense of awe and dread washed over her as she approached. She had found it—the sanctuary Kaelen had spoken of.

The entrance was framed by two towering stone pillars, their surfaces etched with intricate symbols she couldn't begin to understand. The air around the structure hummed with power, the magic in the air stronger here than it had been anywhere else in the forest. It felt as though the very ground beneath her feet was alive, its pulse in sync with her own.

Taking a hesitant step forward, Elara reached out to touch the door, her fingers grazing the cool stone. As her hand made contact, a shock of electricity shot through her, sending a jolt of magic racing up her arm. She gasped, stepping back, but the door creaked open of its own accord, as though it had been waiting for her.

Her heart raced as she stepped inside.

The sanctuary was vast, its interior lit by an eerie, otherworldly glow that seemed to emanate from the walls themselves. The air was thick with magic, and the temperature dropped sharply, sending a chill through her bones. The space was empty, save for a single pedestal in the center of the room, upon which lay a book—a tome bound in dark leather, its pages stained with time.

Elara approached the pedestal slowly, the weight of the moment pressing down on her. She could feel the power of the sanctuary pulsing around her, drawing her closer, urging her to take the book, to open it. But as her fingers hovered over the cover, a sense of dread washed over her. This was no ordinary book—it was a key, a portal to something far darker than she had ever imagined.

Her heart pounded in her chest as she reached out, her hand

trembling. She had come this far. She had no choice but to see this through. She opened the book, the pages creaking in protest, and as she turned the first page, the sanctuary seemed to come alive. The walls trembled, and the air crackled with energy. Symbols glowed on the pages, their meanings shifting and changing before her eyes, and Elara's mind screamed at her to stop, to turn away.

But it was too late.

The power within her surged, and the sanctuary seemed to collapse inward on itself. The ground shook violently beneath her feet, the walls closing in like a prison. She could feel the curse—the ancient magic—rising around her, closing in, suffocating her.

"Elara!" a voice cried out, but it was not Kaelen's. The voice was ancient, hollow, and familiar. It was the voice of the curse itself.

She gasped, the room spinning around her, and before she could react, the world went black.

Ten

The Veil of Deception

Elara's senses were overwhelmed by the darkness. It wasn't just the absence of light, but the suffocating, almost oppressive weight of the blackness that seemed to press against her chest, making it difficult to breathe. She couldn't move. Her limbs felt heavy, as though shackled by invisible chains. The last thing she remembered was the book, the ancient tome, and the way its pages seemed to burn with power as they shifted beneath her fingers. Then, there had been a sudden, deafening silence—and everything had gone black.

Now, she was somewhere else—somewhere not quite real. The air was thick and still, the only sound her own ragged breathing. She tried to raise her hand, but it felt as though the very act of movement was an impossible task. The space around her stretched out infinitely, but there was no sense of distance. The air was cold, unnaturally cold, and a chill crept down her spine as she strained her eyes against the darkness.

"Elara..." The voice was a whisper, so faint at first that she wasn't sure if it was real. But it came again, clearer this time, and it sent a shiver down her entire body. "Elara..."

She tried to speak, to call out, but her mouth was dry, her words trapped inside her throat. The voice—was it Kaelen?—called her name once more, and this time it was unmistakable. But there was something off about it, something distant, hollow. Her heart raced, and she forced her legs to move, desperate to find the source.

"Elara..."

The voice seemed to come from everywhere and nowhere, echoing in the emptiness. Panic clawed at her chest, and she stumbled forward, her hands reaching out, but there was nothing to grasp, nothing to anchor her in this void. Her breath grew quicker, more erratic, as the tension in the air thickened, pressing in on her from all sides.

Suddenly, the darkness began to shift. It twisted, the shadows pulling back like a curtain, revealing an expanse bathed in a dim, flickering light. The space around her began to solidify, though its edges seemed to ripple like water. It was as though she were standing on the precipice of two worlds, the real and the imagined, connected by the thinnest of veils. In the distance, she could see a figure—a shadow, indistinct but familiar.

"Elara, you've come."

The Forsaken King's Enchanted Bride

The words chilled her to the bone, and Elara's pulse thundered in her ears as she took a tentative step forward. She wasn't sure what she expected, but the figure that emerged from the gloom was not Kaelen. It was a woman—a dark-haired woman with eyes that gleamed like black pearls, her skin pale, almost translucent. Her face was beautiful, yet there was something unnerving about it, a coldness that made Elara's stomach churn.

The woman smiled, but it didn't reach her eyes. "I see you've found your way here," she said softly, her voice smooth and melodious, yet carrying an unsettling edge.

Elara took a step back, her instinct screaming at her to run. "Who are you?" she demanded, though her voice wavered with uncertainty. "Where am I?"

The woman tilted her head, studying her with those black eyes that seemed to pierce right through her. "I am who you've been seeking. The one who holds the answers to the curse. The one who can guide you." She took a step forward, her presence growing stronger, more oppressive. "You've been searching for something, haven't you, Elara?"

Elara took another step back, her mind racing. "The sanctuary," she breathed, as though the word had been whispered to her. "I was searching for the sanctuary… and the truth."

The woman smiled again, and this time it seemed a little more genuine, though still lacking warmth. "Ah, yes. The truth. But tell me, Elara," she said, her voice turning cold, "are you ready to face it? To see what lies beneath the veil you've been hiding behind?"

Elara's heart clenched, and she swallowed hard. "What do you mean?" she asked, her voice barely more than a whisper. The weight of the words pressed on her, and she suddenly felt the weight of the entire world pressing down on her, like a mountain.

The woman's smile widened, and she raised a hand, her fingers trailing through the air as though weaving invisible threads. "You've lived your life believing one thing, Elara, but the truth is far more complex. The curse is not what you think. The curse is you."

The words hit her like a blow to the chest, and Elara staggered back, her breath coming in short, sharp bursts. "No," she whispered, shaking her head in disbelief. "That's not true."

"Oh, but it is," the woman replied, her voice dripping with cold amusement. "The curse is not something that was placed upon you. It is not a punishment for something you did. It is a part of you, woven into your very essence. You've always had this power, Elara. You were born with it. The magic within you is older than time, older than the curse itself."

"No," Elara gasped, shaking her head furiously, her hands curling into fists. "I'm not—this isn't me." She stumbled back, her mind spinning. It couldn't be true. She couldn't be the key to the curse, couldn't be tied to it in this way. "I—I can't be…"

The woman's smile deepened, and her eyes glittered with

something cruel. "You've been running from the truth, but you can't outrun it forever. The moment you touched the book in the sanctuary, you sealed your fate. You are the one who holds the power to end this—and to become the source of its destruction."

Elara's legs trembled beneath her, and she collapsed to her knees, her hands pressed against the cold stone beneath her. "What are you talking about?" she breathed, her voice hollow. "What is this power? What do you want from me?"

The woman stepped closer, her shadow stretching long across the ground. "What I want from you, Elara, is simple. The same thing that Kaelen wants. The same thing that I want." She knelt beside Elara, her voice dropping to a whisper. "You must choose. You must choose whether to embrace your true nature or reject it. Whether to wield the magic within you or let it consume you."

Elara's mind reeled. The words, the weight of them, pressed down on her chest like a vice. She had thought she could control this—this power that had been growing inside her, pulsing with life. But now... now she wasn't sure she could even trust her own mind.

The woman's hand reached out, her fingers brushing Elara's cheek, and the touch was like ice. "You can either be the salvation of this world... or its ruin."

Elara's breath caught in her throat as she looked up at the woman. "And Kaelen?" she whispered. "What about Kaelen? Is he part of this?"

The woman's smile flickered, but she said nothing. Instead, she stood and stepped back, her form becoming less distinct, as though she were fading into the very air around them. "The time is near, Elara," she said, her voice drifting away like a memory. "Choose wisely, for your decision will be the one that shapes everything."

And then, with a final whisper, she was gone.

Elara sat there, alone in the dark void, her mind reeling. She had felt the truth in the woman's words, had seen the path laid out before her. But now, as the weight of the decision settled on her shoulders, she understood that the hardest choice lay ahead of her.

The curse had always been inside her, and now she had to decide whether to embrace it—whether to become the thing that could either save or destroy the world.

And the choice was hers alone.

Eleven

The Fallen Kingdom

The sky was bruised, a swirling mass of dark clouds and flashes of lightning that tore through the heavens like jagged knives. The wind howled in the trees, whipping the branches around like frantic, wild dancers. Elara stood on the edge of a cliff, staring down at the valley below where the ruins of the fallen kingdom sprawled like the remains of a long-forgotten dream. The land was twisted, scarred by ancient battles, its fields overrun with dark magic that seemed to pulse with a life of its own. It was a land consumed by loss—a kingdom that had once stood tall and proud, now crumbled beneath the weight of time and power.

It was here that everything had begun.

Her heart raced as she took a step forward, the mist from the valley rising to meet her, wrapping around her legs like a silent, suffocating embrace. She could feel the magic of the land seeping into her bones, the curse that had haunted Kaelen for so long tightening around her like invisible chains. The power in her blood was undeniable now, but it wasn't the kind of magic that flowed freely; it was dark, twisted, and it clung to her like a stain that refused to wash away.

"Kaelen," she whispered, but there was no answer. She was alone now—alone with the remnants of a kingdom that had once been whole, now shattered, forgotten.

She closed her eyes, breathing in the cold, damp air, and for a moment, the world around her seemed to fade. The cries of the past, the echoes of battle, the weight of lost souls—they all merged into a single, haunting memory. She could hear Kaelen's voice, a tortured whisper in her ear, but when she opened her eyes, he was still gone.

The image of the woman from the sanctuary flashed in her mind. The one who had claimed to be the source of the curse, the one who had told her to choose. Elara could feel the weight of that decision pressing down on her like a mountain. Her hands trembled as she clenched them into fists, trying to push the fear away, but it lingered, biting at her resolve.

The wind shifted, the cold air biting at her skin, and she turned toward the ruins below. The kingdom had once been the heart of Kaelen's power, the seat of his throne. Now, it was little more than a broken memory. The once-proud walls of the castle were crumbling, their stones scattered across the land like discarded toys. What had happened here? What had torn this kingdom apart?

A sharp, sudden sound broke through her thoughts—a branch snapping, followed by the heavy crunch of footsteps. She spun around, her hand instinctively reaching for the dagger at her side. Her heart pounded in her chest as she scanned the surrounding trees, searching for the source of the noise. She wasn't alone.

And then, from the shadows of the trees, a figure emerged.

It was him.

Kaelen.

Her breath caught in her throat. He stepped forward, his cloak billowing in the wind, his golden eyes glinting with a mixture of pain and rage. His face was drawn, his features more haggard than she remembered, as though the weight of the world had aged him beyond his years. The curse had taken its toll on him—she could see it in the dark shadows beneath his eyes, in the way he moved, like a man burdened by some unspeakable secret.

"Kaelen," she breathed, her voice trembling. She wanted to run to him, to throw herself into his arms and beg him to come back, to return to the man she had once known. But she held herself back, her mind a whirlwind of conflicting emotions. She didn't know if she could trust him anymore. The curse had changed him.

"Elara," his voice was hoarse, as though it had been a long time since he'd spoken. "You shouldn't have come here."

She took a step forward, her hands clenched into fists at her sides. "I had to. I need to understand. What happened here? What's going on, Kaelen?"

He shook his head slowly, his eyes darkening. "You don't understand," he said, his voice tight with barely restrained emotion. "This kingdom is lost. There's nothing here for you. It's all been destroyed."

"I know it's been destroyed," she snapped, her voice sharp with frustration. "But why? What happened to you, Kaelen? What happened to this place?"

He took a slow step toward her, his eyes filled with something—regret? Pain? She couldn't tell. "The curse wasn't just something that was cast on me. It was meant to destroy everything. Everything I loved. Everything I was supposed to protect."

Elara's heart sank, the weight of his words pressing down on her like a crushing weight. "The curse... it's been controlling you this whole time?"

Kaelen's face tightened, his gaze dark and distant. "Not just controlling me. It's been feeding off my fear, my rage. The more I tried to fight it, the more it took. It destroyed my kingdom, Elara. It destroyed my people."

Elara felt a wave of sorrow wash over her as the realization hit her. Kaelen hadn't chosen this. He hadn't been the one to bring the curse upon his people—it had been forced upon him, a darkness that had consumed him slowly, piece by piece.

"I never wanted this," Kaelen continued, his voice strained. "I never wanted to be the king. I never wanted to wield the power that would end up destroying everything I cared about."

Elara's chest tightened as she stepped closer to him. "Then why didn't you let me help you?" she asked softly. "Why didn't you trust me?"

He looked at her then, really looked at her, and for a moment, there was a flicker of something in his eyes—something almost human. "I didn't want you to suffer the way I did," he said, his voice breaking. "I couldn't let you become a part of this. I couldn't bear the thought of you being caught in the middle of the curse."

She shook her head, her hand reaching out toward him. "But I am part of this. I always have been. I'm not just a bystander in this, Kaelen. I've been connected to it since the beginning."

His expression hardened, and he stepped back, as though her words had pushed him away. "You don't know what you're asking, Elara," he said, his voice low and pained. "The curse doesn't just claim the kingdom. It claims everything. It pulls you in until there's nothing left of you. And I can't let that happen to you."

Her throat tightened as she watched him, her heart aching. She knew he was trying to protect her, but she also knew that this wasn't something she could walk away from. She had to face the truth, whatever it was.

"I don't want to run from it anymore," she said, her voice firm. "I can't. I need to know what happened here, Kaelen. I need to know what we can do to stop it."

Kaelen's eyes flicked to the ruined kingdom below, his gaze distant, as though he were seeing things that weren't there. "You think it's that simple?" he whispered. "You think we can just walk away from the past, from everything that's been lost?"

"I don't know," Elara admitted, her voice breaking. "But I have to try. We have to try."

For a long moment, neither of them spoke, the wind howling around them, carrying the scent of ashes and lost dreams. Finally, Kaelen turned away, his shoulders sagging with the weight of everything he had been carrying for so long.

"You're right," he said quietly. "There's nothing left to lose. But if we're going to do this, we have to face the truth. The heart of the curse is here, Elara. In this kingdom. And we can't stop it until we uncover everything."

Her pulse quickened. She had known this moment would come, but standing here, on the precipice of Kaelen's past, facing the remnants of a kingdom destroyed by magic and rage, she felt the enormity of what they had to do. There was no turning back now.

With a deep breath, Elara stepped forward, determination filling her chest. "Then let's face it together."

Kaelen turned to her, his gaze hardening, the burden of his past still weighing heavily on him. But there was something else in his eyes now—something flickering between the shadows.

The battle for the kingdom, for their future, was far from over. And it was about to begin again.

Twelve

The Sacrifice

The air felt suffocating, thick with the remnants of magic that crackled around them, clinging to their skin, wrapping around their bodies like a net. Elara's breath came in shallow gasps as she stood before the entrance to the hidden chamber, the door made of ancient stone and inscribed with glowing runes. The symbols pulsed with a rhythm that seemed to echo in time with her heartbeat, as though the very earth beneath her feet was alive, watching, waiting.

Kaelen stood beside her, his eyes flicking nervously toward the door, his hand clenched at his side. His jaw was tight, his features etched with a mixture of determination and fear. The tension between them had grown unbearable, each moment stretching out like an eternity. They had come so far, yet she could feel the weight of something far darker looming ahead, a decision that neither of them was ready to make.

"Do you understand what this means?" Kaelen's voice was barely a whisper, as though the words were too heavy to be spoken aloud. He turned to face her, his golden eyes searching hers, a silent plea in the depths of them. "The choice you make here will change everything."

Elara swallowed, the gravity of his words settling over her like a heavy cloak. She had always known that the curse would demand a price, but now, standing here in the ruins of a kingdom that had once been Kaelen's, she could feel the price she would have to pay for the truth. It wasn't just her life at risk anymore. It was his as well.

"I don't know if I can do this," Elara admitted, her voice trembling. The fear, the uncertainty, it was clawing at her chest, squeezing the air from her lungs. "Kaelen, what if we fail? What if this curse... it consumes us both?"

Kaelen's gaze softened, but there was an unreadable edge to his expression. He reached out and took her hand, the warmth of his touch grounding her in the moment. His fingers wrapped around hers with an intensity that spoke volumes. "We don't have a choice anymore," he said quietly. "We've come too far. If we don't stop it now, the curse will claim us all. Every soul in this kingdom. The lives of those who followed me, those who were lost in this war, will be nothing but ashes in the wind."

Elara nodded, but even as the words passed her lips, she knew they didn't quite reach the heart of what she feared. The power she carried inside her, the one she had spent so long trying to understand, felt more like a curse than a gift. Every time she

The Sacrifice

tried to control it, to make sense of it, it slipped further from her grasp. And now, as they stood at the edge of this final step, she could feel the weight of it, pressing down on her like an iron shackle.

She glanced back at the doorway. Beyond it lay the heart of the curse—its source, its beginning. She could sense the magic pulsing from within, an almost tangible force that beckoned her, but at the same time, warned her away. The stones surrounding the door were etched with symbols, some familiar, others foreign. They glowed in the low light, pulsing with a steady rhythm, as though the heart of the kingdom itself was beating.

"You don't have to do this, Elara," Kaelen said, his voice raw, filled with a desperation she had never heard before. "I can go in alone. I can... sacrifice myself. The curse—it's mine to bear. It was always mine. You shouldn't be caught in this."

Elara turned sharply toward him, her pulse spiking. The very thought of Kaelen sacrificing himself was too much to bear. She had already lost him once, to the curse, to the weight of the crown. She couldn't let him do this—not again.

"No," she said, shaking her head fiercely. "You don't get to make that decision for me. I'm not going to stand aside while you sacrifice yourself for something that's beyond both of us." Her voice was steadier than she felt, but there was a fierce fire in her chest now, a clarity that she hadn't had before. "We do this together. We end this together."

Kaelen's expression faltered, and for a brief moment, Elara saw the raw pain behind his eyes. His fingers tightened around hers, but he didn't pull away. Instead, he stepped closer, his breath coming in shallow bursts.

"I don't want you to become part of this," Kaelen whispered. His voice cracked. "The magic inside you… it's changing you, Elara. You're becoming something I can't protect you from."

Her heart thudded painfully in her chest. "I've always been part of it, Kaelen. The power inside me, the magic—it's tied to this. I've been running from it, but I can't anymore." She took a deep breath. "We both know this curse doesn't just live in me. It lives in you too. And until we face it, we're both going to keep drowning in it."

For a moment, the two of them stood there, locked in an unspoken understanding. The weight of everything they had gone through, everything that had brought them here, hung between them. Elara had never felt so connected to Kaelen, nor so utterly torn apart by the reality of what was about to unfold. The decision they faced, the choice that lay before them, was not one they could undo. There would be no turning back once they crossed the threshold of that door.

"I know," Kaelen said quietly, his voice steady now, though the tension in his jaw was still palpable. "But if we fail, Elara…" He trailed off, unable to finish the thought.

Elara squeezed his hand, her pulse steadying. "Then we fail together. But we won't. I won't let you sacrifice yourself alone. Not when we're in this together."

The Sacrifice

Kaelen nodded slowly, and for the first time, the darkness that had clouded his expression seemed to lift, if only for a moment. There was a flicker of hope in his eyes, the smallest hint of the man he used to be—the man she had once believed in completely. It was enough to steady her resolve.

They stood there in silence for a moment longer, the weight of the decision pressing on them, but neither spoke. The world around them felt impossibly still, the oppressive weight of magic hanging heavy in the air. Finally, Kaelen nodded toward the door.

"Are you ready?" he asked, his voice low.

Elara turned to the door, her heart thundering in her chest. The symbols on the stone seemed to shift and shimmer as she stepped closer, the pulse of the magic growing stronger with every step. She could feel it—the curse, the power that had consumed Kaelen for so long, was waiting for them on the other side. The question now was whether they could survive it.

She nodded, her voice barely a whisper. "I'm ready."

Together, they stepped toward the door, and as their hands reached for the stone, the air crackled with raw power. The door swung open slowly, the ancient hinges groaning in protest as they entered the chamber beyond.

Inside, the room was vast, its ceiling stretching high above them, lost in the shadows. The walls were lined with shelves of ancient books, their pages yellowed and fragile with age. In the center of the room stood a pedestal, the object that held the key to the curse—the source of everything. Atop it rested a crystal, its surface glowing with an eerie, otherworldly light. It pulsed in time with Elara's heartbeat, each pulse growing louder and more insistent.

Kaelen stepped forward, his hand outstretched, but Elara stopped him with a hand on his arm. She could feel the power in the air, the way it tugged at her, drawing her in.

"We have to be careful," she said, her voice thick with tension. "Whatever this is, it's waiting for us."

Kaelen nodded, his eyes locked on the crystal. "Whatever happens, Elara… promise me you'll stay with me."

"I'm not going anywhere," she whispered.

Together, they moved toward the pedestal, their hearts racing, the weight of their choice hanging between them. The moment they touched the crystal, the world around them seemed to explode in a wave of light and sound. The room trembled, the walls cracking as the air was filled with the deafening roar of magic being unleashed.

And in that moment, Elara knew that nothing would ever be the same again.

Thirteen

The Dark Heart

Elara's hands trembled as she gripped the pedestal, the crystal pulsing in her palms like a living thing. The room around her felt alive, vibrating with raw, untamed power. The walls, once dark and silent, now seemed to hum, their very stones quivering with energy. The pulse of the crystal matched the frantic beat of her heart, a rhythm that seemed to reverberate through her entire body, sending waves of heat through her veins.

Kaelen stood beside her, his presence a quiet anchor in the chaos that swirled around them. His golden eyes were locked on the crystal, his expression a mixture of awe and fear. For a moment, the two of them simply stood there, hands on the pedestal, as the world seemed to hold its breath. The air crackled, thick with magic, and every fiber of Elara's being screamed at her to pull away.

But she couldn't. She wouldn't.

The power of the crystal was undeniable, a force that called to her, pulling her deeper into its grasp. It was not just a curse. It was the curse—the very source of everything that had brought them here. She could feel its pull, its hunger, as though the crystal itself were feeding off of her, using her to become something more.

"Elara…" Kaelen's voice broke through her thoughts, low and strained. "We need to be careful. This… this is more dangerous than we thought."

She turned her gaze toward him, and for the first time, she saw the fear in his eyes—real fear, not the cold mask he had worn for so long. It sent a chill through her chest. This wasn't just about breaking the curse. It wasn't just about freeing Kaelen from the chains that had bound him for so long. It was about something far darker.

The crystal pulsed again, brighter this time, the light searing into her vision. She tried to step back, to pull away, but the energy that surged through her was too strong, too overwhelming. She felt the pull of it deep in her core, felt the magic inside her stretch and strain in response. She could feel her own power—the same power that had been growing inside her, the same power that had terrified her—rising up in a violent wave, clashing with the curse, as if they were two opposing forces, each desperate to consume the other.

"Elara!" Kaelen's voice rose in panic. He reached out for her, but the force of the magic between them was too strong. The air thickened, twisting into something almost tangible, and she could feel her body being torn in two, caught between the crystal and the curse.

A scream—her scream—ripped from her throat as the magic began to overwhelm her, drowning her in its heat. The room spun around her, the walls warping, the ceiling twisting into a vortex of light and shadow. She couldn't breathe. She couldn't think. The world was collapsing, folding in on itself, and all she could hear was the pulse of the crystal, louder now, deafening, as if it were trying to tear her apart from the inside.

"Kaelen!" she gasped, her voice barely a whisper, swallowed by the roar of the magic. "I can't—"

And then, everything stopped.

The light—the pulse—everything ceased in an instant, as though the world had suddenly been frozen in time. Elara gasped for air, her body shaking, every muscle straining as she tried to break free of the hold the magic had on her. Her fingers were numb from gripping the pedestal, her body trembling from the force of the energy that had surged through her.

Kaelen was beside her, his hands on her shoulders, his face pale, his expression stricken. "Elara," he breathed, his voice a strangled whisper. "Are you... Are you alright?"

She nodded, though she wasn't sure if she believed it herself. The world around her still felt off-kilter, as if she were standing on the edge of something, teetering between two realities. The magic still hummed in the air, but it was… different now. The crystal, once so bright, now pulsed with a dim, steady glow, as though it were waiting for something—or someone.

But the silence that had followed the eruption of magic was broken by something else—a sound. A faint whisper, like a sigh, drifting through the room, carried on the edges of the still air.

"Elara…"

Her blood ran cold. The voice—soft, familiar, but not Kaelen's—was like a breath on the back of her neck. She turned quickly, her eyes scanning the dark room. The air was thick with a presence—something that wasn't quite human, but something that felt ancient, primordial, like a shadow stretching across time.

And then, standing at the edge of the room, as though it had materialized from the darkness itself, was a figure. It was tall, cloaked in shadow, the outlines of its form barely visible. The face was hidden beneath a hood, but even without seeing its features, Elara could feel the weight of its gaze. It was like being watched by something beyond mortal comprehension.

"Elara," the voice whispered again, this time clearer, more tangible. "I've been waiting for you."

Kaelen stepped forward, his body tense, his hand reaching for the blade at his side. "Who are you?" he demanded, his voice low and dangerous.

The Dark Heart

The figure didn't respond immediately. Instead, it stepped closer, its movements fluid, almost unnatural, as if it were gliding through the air. Elara's pulse quickened, the hair on the back of her neck standing on end. There was something about the figure, something about its presence, that made her blood run cold.

"You don't recognize me?" the figure said, its voice now smooth, its tone mocking. "I thought you'd remember me by now."

It raised its hood, revealing a face—pale, gaunt, and unblinking, with eyes that glimmered like black pools of ink. Elara's breath caught in her throat. The figure before her wasn't a stranger. It wasn't just some unknown enemy. No, it was someone she had seen before—someone whose presence had haunted her thoughts since the very beginning.

Dorian.

The truth hit her like a wave, crashing over her with the force of an ocean. She had been searching for answers, but this—this was not what she had expected. Dorian, the man who had once been her ally, was standing before her, his twisted grin spreading across his face as he took another step forward.

"Dorian…" Elara whispered, the name tasting foreign on her tongue. "What are you doing here?"

His smile widened, his black eyes glinting with dark amusement. "What am I doing here? I'm simply here to finish what I started, Elara." His voice was smooth, like silk, but there was no warmth in it. Only the cold bite of truth. "You think you can stop it? The curse? The magic? It's already too late."

Kaelen's grip tightened on his sword, but Dorian waved a dismissive hand. "Don't waste your energy, Kaelen," he said, his voice dripping with disdain. "You're not the one who can stop this. None of you can. You're all part of it now."

Elara took a step back, her mind reeling. "What do you mean, part of it?" she demanded. "What are you talking about?"

Dorian's smile deepened, the cruel glint in his eyes sharp. "You, Elara, are not the answer. You never were. The magic inside you—inside both of you—is not something you can control. It is the darkness that binds you, the very force that destroyed this kingdom." He gestured to the ruins around them, his voice growing colder, more forceful. "The truth is, Elara, you've always been a part of the curse. And now, you'll either join it… or become its sacrifice."

Elara's chest tightened as the weight of his words settled over her like a lead blanket. She looked to Kaelen, his face a mask of fury, but even he seemed unsure, as if the truth of what Dorian said resonated in a place deeper than either of them could admit.

"You can't have her," Kaelen growled, his voice low, full of a raw emotion Elara hadn't heard from him before.

Dorian tilted his head, his eyes flashing with amusement. "I already have her, Kaelen," he said softly, his voice like ice. "And you're too late to stop it."

The tension in the room was palpable now, thick with magic, with secrets, with lies that had long been buried. Elara's mind raced, but it was impossible to keep up with the storm of emotions that churned inside her. She had wanted answers, had needed them—but now that they were within reach, she wasn't sure she could bear them.

As Dorian stepped closer, the room seemed to close in around them, the walls closing off any escape. Elara's breath caught in her throat, her hands shaking at her sides. She was trapped. They were all trapped.

And in that moment, Elara realized the terrible truth: the curse wasn't just a power that sought to destroy them—it was something far worse. It was a force that fed on their fears, their doubts, and their sacrifices.

And now, it was demanding the ultimate price.

Fourteen

The Breaking Point

The air was thick with the scent of decay, a staleness that clung to the stone walls and weighed heavily on Elara's chest. The dark heart of the kingdom was a tomb now—a hollowed-out shell of what it once was. The pulse of magic, that ancient, hungry force that had guided them here, had not lessened since Dorian's arrival. If anything, it had grown stronger, wrapping itself around her like chains, dragging her deeper into the web of lies and betrayal that had been spun around her from the moment she stepped into this cursed land.

She felt the weight of it all—Kaelen's curse, the truth about her blood, the impossible choice between saving the man she loved and destroying the very power that bound him. Dorian's presence here, his words, were a constant reminder that there was no easy way out of this. They were all pawns in a game

The Breaking Point

they hadn't even known they were playing.

And it was almost time for the final move.

Elara's fingers tightened around the hilt of her dagger as she stood at the threshold of the inner sanctum, the chamber where the very heart of the curse lay. The room was vast, dark, and eerily silent. Only the soft hum of magic filled the space, reverberating through the stone walls, vibrating in her bones. In the center of the room stood a large altar, and atop it lay a crystal—a dark, jagged thing, black as night, pulsing with an unnatural light. It was the source, Elara knew it without question. The thing that had brought the curse to Kaelen, to the kingdom, to them all.

The moment she stepped into the chamber, the air seemed to crackle, like static before a storm. The temperature dropped, the shadows growing long, reaching out toward her. Every instinct in her screamed at her to turn back, to flee from this place, but she couldn't. She had come too far to turn away now.

Beside her, Kaelen stood motionless, his eyes locked on the altar, his face a mask of grim determination. He hadn't said much since their encounter with Dorian, and she could feel the tension between them, the unspoken words hanging in the air like a thick fog. But there was something else in his eyes now—something deeper than the curse, than the magic, than the pain. It was a longing, a desperation, that Elara couldn't ignore.

"Elara…" His voice was a whisper, barely audible over the hum of the magic in the room. She turned to him, her heart catching in her chest. His eyes met hers, filled with a mixture of pain and fear. "If we do this... If we break the curse, there's no going back. You know that, don't you?"

She nodded slowly, the weight of his words settling over her like a heavy cloak. The choice she had to make was no longer about saving Kaelen. It was about the kingdom, the people who had suffered because of this curse, and the cost of stopping it. The price would be steep—too steep for her to comprehend fully. But there was no other choice.

She stepped closer to him, her hand reaching out to brush his arm. His gaze softened, but only for a moment. Then he turned back to the altar, his face hardening again.

"I never wanted to bring you into this, Elara," he said, his voice thick with regret. "I never wanted you to carry the burden of this curse, to carry the weight of what it's done to me. But now... now it's too late. We're too far gone."

"Elara, Kaelen, it's time." The voice was Dorian's, cold and mocking, drifting down from the shadows behind them. Elara froze, her heart skipping a beat. She hadn't heard him enter, but there he stood, his figure emerging from the darkness like a predator, his smile twisted with dark amusement. His eyes gleamed like black marble, watching them with a mixture of curiosity and contempt.

"You don't have to do this," Dorian continued, his voice smooth, but laced with menace. "You can walk away now. You can let me take care of it. All of it. You don't need to carry this burden anymore."

Elara spun around, her dagger in her hand, her heart pounding in her chest. She didn't trust him—she never had. But hearing him speak, seeing the smug expression on his face, it only fueled her resolve. The power, the curse, the crystal—it was all connected to him. The lies he had spun, the manipulation, it all led back to him. She would stop him, no matter the cost.

"No," she said, her voice firm, resolute. "We've come this far. There's no turning back."

Dorian's smile faltered, just for a moment, but it was enough to show the cracks in his façade. "You think you're in control here?" he scoffed. "You think you're ready to face the consequences of your actions?"

Kaelen stepped forward, his hand hovering near the sword at his side. "We've made our choice, Dorian. You can't stop us."

For a moment, Dorian's eyes flicked to Kaelen, and something cold and calculating flashed across his face. "You really think you can end it all by touching that crystal?" He laughed, the sound low and cruel. "The curse is not just a spell, Kaelen. It is a part of you. It always has been. You can't escape it."

Kaelen's gaze hardened, his posture shifting with the weight of the truth that Dorian's words carried. Elara felt it too—the pull of the curse, the truth of Dorian's words, like a rope tightening around their throats.

But she couldn't afford to doubt now. Not when they were so close.

"Elara," Kaelen said, his voice tight, his eyes locking with hers. "We can't undo what's been done. But we can stop it. We can stop it from claiming anyone else. If you're ready… I need you to make the choice now."

The words hit her like a stone sinking into her chest, the weight of them pressing down on her with an unbearable force. She could feel the power inside her, the magic that had been awakening, surging in response. It was stronger than ever, and it was begging to be used. But at what cost?

"Elara." Kaelen's voice was softer now, almost a plea. He reached out, his hand brushing hers. "Trust me. Trust us."

And in that moment, she knew. She knew what she had to do.

She stepped toward the altar, her hand trembling as she reached for the crystal. As her fingers brushed the cold surface, the room seemed to explode with light—brilliant, blinding, impossible to look at. A roar of magic filled the room, deafening, suffocating. It felt as though the world itself was coming apart, as though the very foundation of reality was shaking.

"Elara!" Kaelen shouted, but his voice was lost in the deafening noise. His hand shot out to grab hers, but the force of the magic was too strong. The crystal pulsed, and the world seemed to fragment around her, the air thick with power.

The Breaking Point

The room was no longer solid. The walls, the ceiling, the floor—they all twisted, bending in on themselves. Elara's vision blurred, her head spinning, and the magic surged within her, a wave of energy so intense it nearly knocked her off her feet.

And then, she heard it.

A voice.

Her own.

"No... no..." she whispered, the words caught in her throat. She was screaming—screaming inside her own head—but no sound came. The magic was choking her, suffocating her.

The power—her power—was no longer hers to control. It was slipping away, out of her grasp, spinning out of control. The crystal's light flickered, casting shadows that stretched long across the room, stretching out toward Kaelen, toward her. She could feel it—the weight of the curse closing in around them both.

The ground cracked beneath her feet.

"Elara!" Kaelen shouted, his voice finally cutting through the chaos. He grabbed her arm, his grip tight, but even his touch felt distant, as if she were no longer in control of her own body.

The magic surged again, wild and uncontrollable, and Elara knew, with a sickening certainty, that she had reached the breaking point.

Fifteen

The Final Choice

The air was thick with the smell of ozone, the crackling energy of the magic that had consumed the chamber, twisting and warping the very fabric of the world around Elara. The crystal's light continued to pulse erratically, its glow flickering like the heartbeat of some monstrous creature, drawing the curse's power into a vortex of destruction. The ground beneath her feet shook, cracks spread like veins through the stone floor, and the walls seemed to close in on her, squeezing tighter with every passing second.

"Elara!" Kaelen's voice cut through the chaos, raw with desperation. He was close, but the force of the magic—her own magic—was pushing him away. She could feel the pull of it, the weight of the curse, pulling at her very soul. The world around her was splintering, collapsing in on itself, and she couldn't escape it.

She didn't know how it had happened, how everything had

unravelled so quickly, but the truth was undeniable now. The crystal had awoken something inside her—something far darker than she could have imagined. The power, once a mere whisper in her veins, had now become a raging storm, threatening to tear her apart.

She could feel it, surging through her, tearing at her control. Her vision blurred, the edges of the room warping as if reality itself was bending under the weight of the curse. Kaelen's voice echoed in her ears, but it was distant now, as though it was coming from far away, muffled by the deafening roar of the magic.

"Elara, please!" Kaelen's voice was louder now, closer. "You have to fight it!"

But how could she fight it when it felt like a part of her, like the magic was tied to her heart, her breath, her very existence? She could feel the pull of it, the desire to embrace it, to let it consume her completely. The curse was not just Kaelen's burden; it was hers now too. She had always known that, deep down. But now, as the magic swirled around her like a vortex of destruction, she realized that the choice was no longer about breaking the curse—it was about whether or not she could survive it.

"Elara," Kaelen's voice was close now, urgent, his hands gripping her shoulders, shaking her. "Look at me! You are stronger than this!"

His hands were warm against her skin, and for a moment, the world seemed to stop spinning. Her breath caught in her throat, and she turned her head to look at him, her heart racing in her chest. His eyes were filled with pain, but there was something else there too—something that felt like hope, as if he was still trying to believe that they could make it through this.

"I... I don't know if I can," she whispered, her voice shaky, barely audible above the roaring chaos that filled the room.

"You can," Kaelen insisted, his voice firm. *"You must."*

But his words did little to quell the storm inside her. The power was too strong, too relentless. It was like a tidal wave crashing over her, and she was drowning in it. She could feel the weight of it, the curse pulling her in, dragging her toward the edge. Her hands shook as she tried to hold on to whatever control she had left, but it felt like the magic was slipping through her fingers, too wild, too powerful to contain.

Suddenly, there was a sharp crack—the sound of stone breaking. The pedestal holding the crystal trembled, and the crystal itself began to shake, its light flashing erratically. Elara gasped as a burst of raw energy erupted from the crystal, sending a shockwave through the room. The force of it threw her backward, and she felt herself crashing into the cold stone floor.

For a moment, everything went dark. Her vision swam as she tried to make sense of the world around her. Her head throbbed, and her limbs felt heavy, numb, as though they weren't hers. She struggled to sit up, her hands digging into the ground as she tried to push herself off the floor. But it was no use—the magic was too strong. It had taken over her body, her mind, and now it was trying to claim her very soul.

"Kaelen…" she whispered, her voice barely audible as she looked up. She could see him, standing in front of her, but the world around him seemed to ripple, as if he were fading in and out of focus.

"Elara!" Kaelen shouted, his voice filled with urgency and pain. He reached out for her, but his hand seemed to stretch farther than it should have, the distance between them growing. "You have to *fight* it! Don't let it take you!"

The Final Choice

The words were a lifeline, a tether to reality, but they felt distant, as if they were coming from the other side of a great abyss. Elara's chest tightened as she fought to focus, to see through the haze of magic that clouded her mind. She could feel the curse, the power inside her, gnawing at her from the inside. It wanted her to give in, to surrender to the darkness, to become one with it.

But something in her—something deep within—refused. She couldn't let go. She couldn't give up.

The storm inside her grew, an overwhelming force that clawed at her from every direction. Her body shook, her muscles trembling with the strain of holding on. The magic inside her flared again, more intense now, more dangerous. Her vision blurred, and the edges of the room seemed to shift, bending in impossible angles. She was losing herself.

"Elara!" Kaelen's voice, so full of emotion, broke through the noise. His hand reached out again, this time touching her arm. She could feel the warmth of his touch, the heat of his skin against hers, and it was the only thing that anchored her, that reminded her of who she was.

The world around her seemed to stop, the chaotic energy around her receding just slightly. Her heart pounded, every beat a reminder of the life she had lived before the curse had claimed her, before she had become part of it. She wasn't just some vessel for the curse's power. She wasn't just some pawn in a game between gods and monsters. She was *Elara*. She was *alive*.

With all the strength she could muster, she grabbed Kaelen's hand, holding on tightly as she forced herself to her feet. Her breath came in ragged gasps, but the world around her seemed to quiet, the magic still thrumming beneath the surface, but no longer as all-consuming. For a moment, she felt grounded, like she had regained a small piece of herself.

"Kaelen… I don't know if I can control it," she said, her voice trembling as she held onto him. "I don't know if I can stop it."

Kaelen's eyes were filled with fear, but there was something else there too—a kind of fierce hope, a belief that she could do it. "You don't have to control it, Elara," he said softly, his hand tightening around hers. "You have to *embrace* it. We have to *embrace* it."

The words hit her like a wave, and for the first time, she felt a sense of clarity wash over her. She wasn't alone in this. She wasn't the only one fighting the curse. Kaelen had carried this burden for so long, but now, it was her turn to fight, to stand beside him.

She nodded, feeling the power inside her surge in response. The curse wasn't just something to fight against. It was a part of her, part of the world they both inhabited. And she wasn't going to let it destroy everything.

The crystal pulsed again, its light blinding, but this time, Elara didn't flinch. She held onto Kaelen, her grip firm, and together, they reached out toward the heart of the curse, the source of its power. She could feel it—the magic, the curse, the world around them shifting. But this time, it was different. It wasn't about domination. It was about balance.

As they touched the crystal, the room exploded with light, a burst of raw energy that sent a shockwave through the chamber. Elara's mind reeled, the power rushing through her like a river of fire. The world seemed to shatter, the walls crumbling, the stone cracking beneath their feet. But through it all, she held onto Kaelen, her connection to him steady, unwavering.

The curse had been strong. But together, they were stronger.

www.ingramcontent.com/pod-product-compliance
Lightning Source LLC
LaVergne TN
LVHW020425080526
838202LV00055B/5040